CONTEMPLATING **IRELAND**

Photographs by JAMES GLEASON

Introduced by DEIRDRE PURCELL

ATLANTIC IRELAND

In the beginning was the sea. And then there were stones.

At 1,700 million years, the oldest rock so far discovered in Ireland is on Inishtrahulla, a tiny island off the sea-struck coast of County Donegal in the northwest. Yet to the visitor who comes to Ireland to see, hear and feel what this country is all about, a scientific fact like this is nothing more than data. To a scholar, the language lines of Ogham, etched so precisely in needles of standing stone, call for study toward translation. To the mystic or even the casual tourist their meaning matters less than the personal song of their sculptor.

A round tower may have been built 1,500 years ago as a watchpost and sanctuary against predatory neighbors and foreign invaders but today it stands as a dreamy symbol of a golden monastic past; the Neolithic stone tomb at Newgrange may predate Stonehenge and the pyramids of Egypt but today it is a beacon erected by our ancestors to light our way into lives passed 5,000 years ago.

James Gleason took his photographs during the spring of 1999. Each day he was struck with what we in Ireland take for granted: four seasons in the space of one morning, an entire climate in a day. Even more than the weather, he was struck by the freshly minted quality of the Irish light that caught him at every turn and painted enhanced levels of meaning on every contour.

Yes, we do get a lot of rain but it blows in from the clean expanse of the Atlantic to green the fields. And yes, we do get a lot of wind but it has driven the ocean to carve our cliffs, indent our shorelines and pound our rocks and stones so that our beaches offer sand as fine as bleached flour. Together, the Irish wind, rain and sudden light give us multiple, serial rainbows, dramatic skies—and a hardy population that rejoices communally when the sun comes out.

You will find no city, town or village in Ireland that is not en fete during what we describe as a heatwave—any period of more than two days that produces temperatures higher than 72 degrees Fahrenheit. It is the very unexpectedness of this that causes such a pleasant commotion. Sun umbrellas appear outside pubs. Shorts and sunglasses are sported in sober offices. Parks, beaches, fields, road verges, waste ground, balconies, car lots and all flat surfaces sprout a fungus of white skin turning violently pink because its owners cannot bear to miss a single ray of precious UV. I pray you will live to see it.

The limestone that covers two thirds of our country undoubtedly produces fertile grasslands and strong racehorses but it is the accumulation of uncovered stone; the implacable seacliffs; the moonscape pavements of the Burren; the tumbled, jigsaw walls of Connacht, West Munster and West Ulster; the druidic stone circles, dolmens and ring forts that most invite and then reward contemplation.

These stones tell stories if you have time to sit and listen.

Gleason's landscapes might seem empty at first glance but the moody, black-and-white compositions are full of presences. They seem to articulate a sense of stillness and waiting. He has included few living creatures but where they exist, a few sheep, a lone walker, they seem detached, part of their environment and yet only passing through. Human artifacts—an ancient cloister, a corrugated roof, an abraded Celtic cross—seem to await a return.

His lens, in penetrating the rugged surface of the countryside, seems to give us access to the deeper nature of man, just as the Celts, in common with other ancient cultures, held land to be sacred and that to pierce it physically was to access a spiritual underworld. It is no coincidence that for thousands of years, water wells have been significant in the Irish landscape. Early in the mission to convert, Christian leaders, quick to adapt, appropriated existing water wells as Christian shrines. To this day these wells are associated with local saints, places of pilgrimage where healing is still reputed to take place.

In Ireland we celebrate a poem attributed in legend to Patrick, our patron saint. In these few lines, Patrick not only demonstrates this shrewd bridgebuilding between the Celtic pantheistic preoccupations and the new religion he so successfully promulgated but in expressing it as a chant or incantation, he also appealed to the Celtic love of language. Spells and chants were very important in that ancient world where negativity could be dispelled by invocation. This translation is by the Celtic scholar, Kuno Meyer:

> I ARISE TODAY
> THROUGH THE STRENGTH OF HEAVEN:
> LIGHT OF SUN,
> RADIANCE OF MOON,
> SPLENDOR OF FIRE,
> SPEED OF LIGHTNING,
> SWIFTNESS OF WIND,
> DEPTH OF SEA,
> STABILITY OF EARTH,
> FIRMNESS OF ROCK.

Modern, 21st century Ireland is racing fast. We travel not as mendicant emigrants now, but as prosperous holidaymakers. Our young, confident population picks and chooses from lucrative careers at home in new technology industries. Their parents no longer huddle by turf fires in thatched cottages but trawl the Internet and launch e-companies from bright warm homes and expensive modern apartments. Our cities are spreading, the bustling shopping malls that ring them could be Anywhere, Europe or even Anywhere, USA.

Along with this material prosperity has come attitudinal and religious change of course. The churches are no longer full; for lack of vocations, the monasteries and convents are starting to close; our social and civic laws no longer parallel so closely the moral imperatives of the churches.

Communities have changed too. Some villages and towns have become commuter dormitories while dual carriageways are being cut through forests to accommodate the huge increase in traffic flow. News of our prosperity has spread, and for the first time, we are confronted with travelers from less fortunate parts of the world who beg admission to our feast, an ironic reversal of fortune that seems to have thrown us into some confusion.

Yet James Gleason's photographs tell a continuing truth about our landscape and our nature because beneath the hustle, the spiritual nature of the Irish Celt remains intact. For instance, when the 20th century turned to the 21st, the television transmission most talked about here was the sunset shot from Dursey Sound off the southwest corner of Ireland, an incandescent, salmon-and-gold display that stole the light almost imperceptibly as though recognizing the portent. And the most appreciated official gesture was the distribution by the Irish government of a special candle to each household. While the light faded slowly from this second millennium, these candles were lit across every conurbation and townland to illuminate the darkness until the first dawn of the third.

We still wake our dead and feel we are in communication with them. We modern Europeans and citizens of the world still refuse to cut a highway through an ancient "fairy rath" for fear of offending the inhabitants of an underworld we instinctively feel exists. Although we are no longer the simple peasantry of tradition and Hollywood, we still value and honor the cultures, beliefs and practices of our fathers and ancestors.

When God made time, he made a lot of it, goes the popular Irish saying. You will find this imprinted on tea towels and tacky souvenirs but it is the truth nonetheless.

It takes time to learn the Irish landscape and thereby the Irish character but if you give it time you will get time in return. A lot of it.

— DEIRDRE PURCELL

9

On the bog road the blackthorn flowers, the turf stacks,

Chocolate brown, are built like bricks but softer,

And softer too the west of Ireland sky.

Turf smoke is chalked upon the darker blue

And leaves a sweet, rich poor man's smell in cloth.

—Anthony Cronin

18

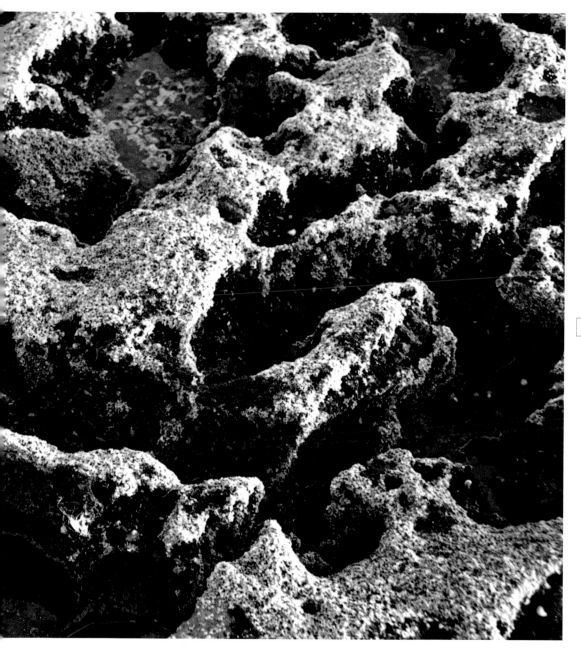

STONY SEABOARD, FAR AND FOREIGN

STONY HILLS POURED OVER SPACE,

STONY OUTCROP OF THE BURREN,

STONES IN EVERY FERTILE PLACE...

—John Betjeman

'I AM OF IRELAND,

AND THE HOLY LAND OF IRELAND

AND TIME RUNS ON,' CRIED SHE.

'COME OUT OF CHARITY,

COME DANCE WITH ME IN IRELAND.'

—W. B. Yeats

A RUINED ABBEY, CHANCEL ONLY,

LICHEN-CRUSTED, TIME-BEFRIENDED

SOARED THE ARCHES, SPLAYED AND SPLENDID,

ROMANESQUE AGAINST THE SKY.

—John Betjeman

I SAVE THE SEED OF THE FIRE TO-NIGHT,

AND SO MAY CHRIST SAVE ME;

ON TOP OF THE HOUSE LET MARY,

IN THE MIDDLE LET BRIGHID BE.

LET EIGHT OF THE MIGHTIEST ANGELS

ROUND THE THRONE OF THE TRINITY,

PROTECT THIS HOUSE AND ITS PEOPLE

TILL THE DAWN OF THE DAY SHALL BE.

—Anonymous

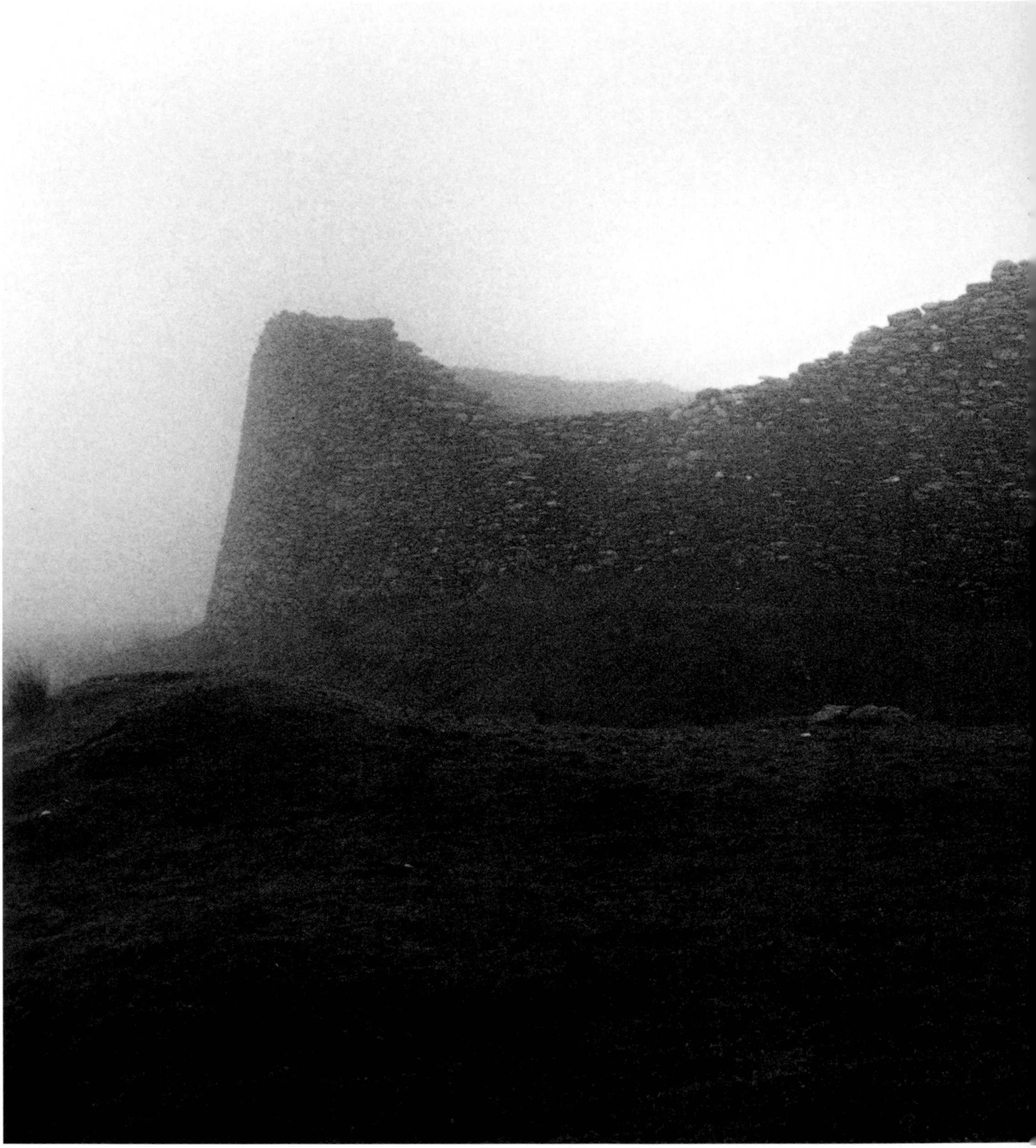

43

I WILL ARISE AND GO NOW, FOR ALWAYS NIGHT AND DAY

I HEAR THE LAKE WATER LAPPING WITH LOW SOUNDS BY THE SHORE;

WHILE I STAND ON THE ROADWAY, OR ON THE PAVEMENTS GREY,

I HEAR IT IN THE DEEP HEART'S CORE.

—W. B. Yeats

In a quiet water'd land, a land of roses,

Stands Saint Kieran's city fair;

And the warriors of Erin in their famous generations

Slumber there.

—T. W. Rolleston

LYING ON THE WARM ROCKS THEY SEE IRELAND

STRETCHED SILENT, ENIGMATIC, APART FROM THEM

AND ARE CONTENT THAT IT IS SO.

THEIR POVERTY IS KNOWN TO MANY,

THEIR WAY OF THOUGHT TO A FEW;

THEY REMAIN MOTIONLESS, ON THE EDGE OF EUROPE,

WITH THE DUST OF SAINTS BENEATH THEIR FEET.

—Somerville and Ross

COME AWAY, O HUMAN CHILD!

TO THE WATERS AND THE WILD

WITH A FAERY, HAND IN HAND,

FOR THE WORLD'S MORE FULL OF WEEPING

THAN YOU CAN UNDERSTAND.

—W. B. Yeats

ON SOME ISLAND I LONG TO BE,

A ROCKY PROMONTORY, LOOKING ON

THE COILING SURFACE OF THE SEA.

TO SEE THE WAVES, CREST ON CREST

OF THE GREAT SHINING OCEAN, COMPOSING

A HYMN TO THE CREATOR, WITHOUT REST.

Colmcille
Version: John Montague

Give thee safe passage on the wrinkled sea,

Himself thy pilot stand,

Bring thee through mist and foam to thy desire,

Again to Irish land.

—Colman
Version: Helen Waddell

ANCIENT IRELAND, INDEED! I WAS REARED BY HER BEDSIDE,

THE RUNE AND THE CHANT, EVIL EYE AND AVERTED HEAD,

FOMORIAN FIERCENESS OF FAMILY AND LOCAL FEUD.

GAUNT FIGURES OF FEAR AND OF FRIENDLINESS,

FOR YEARS THEY TRESPASSED ON MY DREAMS,

UNTIL ONCE, IN A STANDING CIRCLE OF STONES,

I FELT THEIR SHADOWS PASS

INTO THAT DARK PERMANENCE OF ANCIENT FORMS.

—John Montague

THE LOW WALLS OF ROCK-FIELDS IN THE WEST

ARE BEAUTIFUL CLEAN WHITE. THERE ARE CHINKS BETWEEN

THE NEAT WHITE STONES TO LET THE WIND THROUGH SAFE,

YOU CAN SEE THE BLUE SUN THROUGH THEM.

—Pearse Hutchinson

When he stripped off blanket bog

The soft-piled centuries

Fell open like a glib:

There were the first plough-marks,

The stone-age fields, the tomb

Corbelled, turfed and chambered,

Floored with dry turf-coomb.

A landscape fossilized,

Its stone-wall patternings

Repeated before our eyes

In the stone walls of Mayo.

—Seamus Heaney

AND WHERE THE EARTH WAS SOFT FOR FLOWERS WE MADE

A GRAVE FOR HIM THAT HE MIGHT BETTER REST.

SO, SPRING SHALL COME AND LEAVE IT SWEET ARRAYED,

AND THERE THE LARK SHALL TURN HER DEWY NEST.

—Francis Ledwidge

A SHOULDER OF ROCK

STICKS HIGH UP OUT OF THE SEA,

A FISHERMAN'S MARK

FOR LOBSTER AND BLUE-SHARK.

FISSILE AND STARK

THE CRUST IS FLAKING OFF,

SEAL-ROCK, GULL-ROCK,

COVE AND CLIFF.

—Richard Murphy

GAZE NORTH-EAST

OVER HEAVING CREST

WITH SEA PRESS

   CEASELESS:

SEALS' ROAD

FOR SLEEK SPORT

THE TIDE RUN TO

   FULLNESS.

—Anonymous
Version: John Montague

PHOTO CAPTIONS

PAGE 1: Statue detail, Slea Head, County Kerry.

PAGES 2–3: Inishmore, Aran Islands.

PAGES 8–9: Cliffs of Moher, County Clare.

PAGE 10: Freshly harvested turf, Maumturk Mountains, County Galway.

PAGE 12: Sky Road, Clifden, County Galway.

PAGE 13: Gable end, Dingle Peninsula, County Kerry.

PAGE 14–15: Stone walls, Aran Islands.

PAGE 16: Gallarus Oratory, ca. 568–770 AD, Dingle Peninsula, County Kerry.

PAGE 17: East window, Gallarus Oratory.

PAGES 18–19: Doolin Quay, County Clare.

PAGE 21: Beehive hut, ca. 1000 AD, Dunbeg Fort, County Kerry.

PAGES 22–23: Clogher Head, County Kerry.

PAGES 24–25: Croagh Patrick, County Mayo.

PAGE 27: St. Patrick, Ballintubber Abbey, County Mayo.

PAGES 28–29: Clew Bay from Croagh Patrick, County Mayo.

PAGES 30–31: Sheep on the N59, County Mayo.

PAGES 32–33: Roscommon Castle, ca. 1280, County Roscommon.

PAGE 35: Clonmacnois, County Offaly.

PAGES 36–37: Roonah Quay, County Mayo.

PAGE 38: Aillebrack, County Galway.

PAGES 40–41: Staigue Fort, ca. 300 AD, County Kerry.

PAGE 42: Church at Westport House, County Mayo.

PAGE 43: Gallowglass on tomb, Roscommon Abbey, County Roscommon.

PAGES 44–45: Rockfleet Castle, County Mayo.

PAGE 46: Stag Island, County Kerry.

PAGE 48: View of round tower, Clonmacnois, founded 545 AD, County Offaly.

PAGE 49: Crucifixion shrine, Slea Head, County Kerry.

PAGE 50: High cross, ca. 9th century, Clonmacnois.

PAGE 53: View from Dún Aengus, Inishmore, Aran Islands.

PAGE 54: Poulnabrone Dolmen, ca. 3500 BC, County Clare.

PAGES 56–57: Slieveanea, Connor Pass, County Kerry.

PAGE 59: Near Maam Cross, County Galway.

PAGE 60: La-tène Stone, ca. 100 BC, Castlestrange, County Roscommon.

QUOTATION CREDITS

PAGE 61: Graveyard gate, County Clare.

PAGE 62: *Four Masters*, Dingle Harbor, County Kerry.

PAGES 64–65: Roofline, Aran Islands.

PAGE 67: Leamanegh Castle, built 1480, expanded 1640, County Clare.

PAGES 68–69: Blasket Islands, County Kerry.

PAGE 70: Stone wall, County Kerry.

PAGES 72–73: Stone building, County Kerry.

PAGE 75: Clew Bay, County Mayo.

PAGE 76: Ballintubber Abbey, founded 1216, County Mayo.

PAGE 77: St. Patrick and Croagh Patrick.

PAGE 78–79: Ballintubber Abbey.

PAGE 80–81: Macgillycuddy's Reeks, County Kerry.

PAGE 83: Virgin Mary, Ballintubber Abbey.

PAGES 84–85: Burrishoole Abbey, founded 1469, County Mayo.

PAGE 87: Dún Chaoin, County Kerry.

PAGE 88–89: Cliffs of Moher, County Kerry.

PAGE 90: Dingle Peninsula, County Kerry.

PAGES 92–93: Stone wall, County Kerry.

The publisher has made a thorough effort to locate all persons having any rights or interests in material and to clear reprint permissions. If any required acknowledgments have been omitted or any rights overlooked, we regret the error.

PAGE 11: From *R.M.S. Titanic* by Anthony Cronin. By kind permission of the author.

PAGES 20 & 34: From *Ireland with Emily*, by John Betjeman from *Collected Poems*. By kind permission of John Murray (Publishers) Ltd.

PAGE 26: *I Am of Ireland*, Page 47: *The Lake Isle of Innisfree*, Page 55: *The Stolen Child*, by W. B. Yeats. By kind permission of A. P. Watt Ltd., on behalf of Michael B. Yeats. Reprinted with the permission of Scribner, a division of Simon & Schuster, from *The Collected Poems of W. B. Yeats*, Revised Second Edition edited by Richard J. Finneran. Copyright © 1983, 1989 by Anne Yeats.

PAGE 39: From *In Search of Ireland*, H. V. Morton.

PAGE 51: *Clonmacnois*, by R. W. Rolleston.

PAGE 58: Colmcille, version by John Montague © 1998. Permission to reprint granted by Harold Matson Co., Inc. By kind permission of the author and The Gallery Press.

PAGE 66: *Home Again*, by John Montague, *Collected Poems* (1995) by kind permission of the author and The Gallery Press. Reprinted with the permission of Wake Forest University Press.

PAGE 71: *Gaeltacht*, by Pearse Hutchinson, *Selected Poems* (1982) by kind permission of the author and The Gallery Press.

PAGE 74: *Belderg*, by Seamus Heaney from *North*. By kind permission of Faber and Faber Ltd. By kind permission of Farrar Strauss & Giroux.

PAGE 86: *High Island*, by Richard Murphy, *Collected Poems* (2000). By kind permission of the author and The Gallery Press. Reprinted with the permission of Wake Forest University Press.

PAGE 91: *Gaze North-East*, version by John Montague © 1998, permission to reprint granted by Harold Matson Co., Inc. By kind permission of the author and The Gallery Press.

Dora and Charlie's kitchen, County Roscommon.

MANY THANKS FOR THE SUPPORT OF OUR FAMILY AND FRIENDS.
NÍOR EITEALL ÉAN RIAMH AR SCIATHÁN AMHÁIN.

Designed by Mary Parsons
Edited by Andrew Clarke
The photographs in this book were reproduced from gelatin silver prints
by James Gleason and Black & White, Arlington, Virginia.
Quotations as attributed on page 95.

Printed in China through Asia Pacific Offset

8 7 6 5 4 3 2   2008 2007 2006 2005 2004 2003 2002 2001 2000

ISBN 0-9679375-0-7

www.atlanticireland.com
Distributed in the United States by LPC Group, 1-800-626-4330.
Contemplating Ireland Notecards are also available at your local book or gift store.
Contemplating Ireland is available at special bulk discount for promotional
and premium use. Call 1-800-756-4344.